Boundary Waters

BOUNDARY WATERS

Photography by **Jerry Stebbins**
Text by **Greg Breining**

Nodin Press • Minneapolis, Minnesota

*To the memories of Sigurd Olson,
who fought to protect what
little wilderness we have left,
and to my grandfather C. K. Malmin,
who taught me how to fish.*
　　　　　　　　　　—Jerry Stebbins

*To my father, who showed me canoe
country.*
　　　　　　　　—Greg Breining

Photographs ©1983 by Jerry Stebbins. Text ©1983 by Greg Breining. All rights reserved. No part of this book may be produced in any form without the permission of Nodin Press, except for review purposes.

ISBN 0-931714-20-6   First Printing

Nodin Press, a division of Micawber's Inc., 525 North Third Street, Minneapolis, MN 55401.

Printed in U.S.A. at
Litho Specialties, Inc., St. Paul

Contents

Prologue

CANOE COUNTRY—THE BOUNDARY WATERS CANOE AREA WILDERNESS, OFFICIALLY—SITS SMACK AGAINST MINNESOTA'S NORTHERN BORDER ATOP A BIG PLAIN OF ROCK CALLED THE CANADIAN SHIELD. THE ROCK, BRISTLING from the landscape, makes jagged cliffs and huge granite domes, and forms thundering rapids and high falls where it intersects the downward rush of rivers. Nestled between the folds of rock are nearly as many lakes as there are stars on a clear country night. The geography of the land is so intricate one nineteenth-century map maker skipped the detail and simply christened it the "Region of Rocks and Water."

When I took my first trip to the Boundary Waters, I didn't know that the region encompassed some fourteen hundred lakes larger than five acres, that much of the rock was formed more than two billion years ago, that the voyageurs used the lattice-work of water to cross the continent in the eighteenth and nineteenth centuries. All this I would learn later. But I discovered immediately that my imagination, fears, and beliefs all worked together to fashion a spiritual and emotional world from the wilderness. The land seemed to assume a personality and virtue of its own and, like the world of the Ojibway, its early inhabitants, to conceal a ghost in every cliff and churning brook.

I was twelve on that first trip. Dad had spent weeks making plans. He unearthed equipment from a dusty corner of the garage, borrowed the rest, and packed packs. My seven-year-old brother and I loaded sleeping bags, cook pots, and food into our tired blue station wagon. We sped northward from Minneapolis until the freeway turned to highway and the highway to road. The rolling hills and open fields of central Minnesota turned to dark evergreen forest, and then bleak, jagged rock began to sprout from the roadside. We stopped that night in Ely, a vestigial mining town built on a hill of greenstone, whose five thousand people now make their livings by lumbering, pulp cutting, and outfitting trips into the nearby wilderness. Snuggled in a sleeping bag in the back of the station wagon, I imagined more woods than I ever had seen, and my mind played with my father's words: "We might paddle for days without seeing anyone."

With daylight we drove out of town down the Fernberg Road. We launched our canoe, an aluminum seventeen-footer sunk nearly to the gunwales by the weight of Dad in the stern, me in the bow, and my brother squished amidships between nine man-days of food and gear. Dad spread the map across the packs, showed us our route down a chain of lakes, and set a course by compass. We paddled, sometimes clumsily, until we reached the portage into the next lake, which we attacked with great vigor, if little teamwork—an unmanageable amount of gear managed by two kids who had only the slightest idea of what they were doing, and my father, who was the single real beast of burden. We paddled and portaged through the day, until a rising wind chased us into a secluded bay where we found a clearing on a rocky ridge. We pitched a tent and called the site ours.

For two days we watched loons, turtles, and muskrats in the bay, and my brother and I explored the dark, scary woods behind the tent. One afternoon we paddled up the Kawishiwi River until we were stymied by a rapids whose force exceeded our desire to push on. We then turned our attention to a little swamp river and followed it, the creek narrowing and the swamp grasses brushing the canoe, until the channel disappeared in a wide, boggy meadow. We saw deer, and once, I recall, we surprised two moose as they swam across a bay, and we paddled alongside them until they reached shore. Most of all, however, I remember rocks and water, one against the other. A big rapids joined our lake with another, and the water rushed and roared against the boulders and fell into a deep, foam-covered fishing hole. A cliff dropped into the lake near our campsite, breeze-ruffled waves lapping the rock. Nearby, a long point of rock jutted into the lake and slipped below the surface, where it remained visible in the clear water beneath us.

Since that trip years ago, I've often taken my canoe to the lakeside, paddled off, leaving my day-to-day troubles sulking at the portage, and gathered my memories: faint wolf howls on a frosty night; the pale, elusive lights of the aurora borealis; the warm yellow and brown of grasses and forest; and the brilliant white of birches as sunlight tore away thunderheads after a spring rain.

I often have sat on an outcrop next to a big, steep rapids, watching and listening to the whole life of the river crash against the rock. Sometimes I've found the sound reassuring and exciting, as vibrant as the laughter of the Ojibway water spirits. Other times the never-ending drone has seemed as ominous as my own first resonating thought of death. The woods are filled with happiness, sadness, hope, and fear, but none belongs to the wilderness—each is ours. They are the elixir or poison we bring with us. We stand watch over the big lakes, and the cold, silent cliffs echo our own thoughts and let our imaginations run.

Left— Island campsite on Lac la Croix

Granite outcrop on Cypress Lake

Canoe country names, like the land itself, are anchored in bedrock. From east to west along the American-Canadian border are Mountain and Gunflint lakes, then Magnetic Lake, the Granite River, and Gneiss Lake. Farther west is Knife Lake, its shores made of a flinty rock sharp enough to draw blood. Off to the east, just south of the border, is a line of red granite hills called *Misquah*—Ojibway for red. Scattered around the rest of the region are Mesaba Lake (named for the Indian giant of the underground), Iron Lake, Rocky Lake, Red Rock Lake, Gabbro Lake, Jasper Lake, Pipestone Bay, Ledge Lake, Boulder Lake, Boulder Bay, Stone Lake, and Marble Lake.

There is something clean and reassuring about rock—and something awesome, too. We lie on an outcrop at night, the rock sucking heat from our bodies, drawing it into the earth. We shift around on the big slab, trying to find contours to accommodate our backs. Dinner is done, the fire out, the canoes on shore and overturned, the tents set. There is nothing left but to look skyward. Over there, to the north, are Ursa Major and Ursa Minor—the Great and Little bears—the two constellations that comprise the Big Dipper and Little Dipper. Polaris, the North Star, is there, hovering above the earth's pole. Within our sight and imaginations, only these stars are older than the rock against our backs. We know the age of the rock better than we know that of the stars, yet the figures—more than 2.5 billion years for this outcrop of Saganaga granite beneath us—fail to strike to the heart of the

matter. Such an age is incomprehensible—millions of lifetimes. The life of a rock is a long one, its character slow to change.

We are at the southernmost reach of the Canadian Shield, a Precambrian plain of exposed rock that covers nearly two million square miles in a fan-shaped area extending from northern Minnesota into central Canada and northeast around Hudson Bay. The rocks of the Canadian Shield are foundation rocks, among the first formed after the crust of the young earth cooled and wrinkled like the scum on a pot of warm soup. About 2.75 billion years ago, though much of the land was covered by sea, it began to warp and rise with the movement of molten rock deep below. As the earth's crust folded, in places it split, and the magma poured over it. Though this was a time of earthquakes and volcanoes, much of the change must have occurred slowly; had anyone been around to listen, the rumbling deep down in the earth would have been undetectable. The movement, however, gradually brought to the surface the rock that would form canoe country. Great sheets of rock shifted miles against one another, and the entire shield eventually was lifted above sea level.

No one is really sure what happened next. Because no large bodies of water covered the land, few fossils accumulated. There was, nonetheless, life and the lifelike action of the elements. Wind, water, and plant life gnawed at the rock, leveled it, aged it. What lakes there were became rivers by the erosion at their inlets and outlets, or they became bogs and meadows through the deposition of sediment and organic matter. The land, once jagged and hard, became flat or gently rolling, covered by thick forests and drained by old, winding rivers.

Millions of years ago, for reasons still unknown, temperatures began to drop. Though the average temperature was just a few degrees colder than our climate today, the effects were enormous. The polar ice cap began to reach southward, and snow accumulated, intensifying the cold by reflecting more and more of the sun's light. With each new layer of snow, the underlying ice crystals packed together until they interlocked and formed glacier ice, opaque and blue gray from dirt and the absence of air inside the ice mass. Pressure finally made the ice deep below fluid, and two million years ago, the mass of snow and ice began to move across the land. The glaciers may have advanced ten feet one day, ten inches the next, but they moved southward persistently, for only two things can stop a glacier: warm weather or an ocean.

Nearly two miles thick in places, the glaciers stood above the land to the south of them like a giant mesa and pressed down with enough weight to sink the bedrock up to a tenth of a mile. The ice broke the forests into kindling. It tore off and carried away mastodon-sized hunks of rock. The glaciers were always grinding as they proceeded, polishing the bedrock if the abrasive they carried was fine. If the grit was coarse, bedrock was striated in the direction the ice traveled.

Four times glaciers swept the Boundary Waters region. Each time, the scars left by previous glaciers were deepened, ridges flattened. Deposits of sand and gravel were rearranged as a child would scatter sand castles at a beach. When the last glacier crept back to Canada twelve thousand years ago, the system of mature rivers had been destroyed. Instead, the ice left behind craters and trails of drift, basins for thousands of lakes, footprints of the glaciers.

Down by our feet water laps the rock. I begin to count each slap of the waves but soon lose track. How many waves have hit the outcrop since we've been here? A thousand, perhaps. How many more since this land was created? And how much longer still has the rock been here with no waves to strike it?

A meteor flashes. The Big Dipper has turned around the polestar like a watch hand of the night. The old beneath us, the truly ancient far above, we now search the black sky for passing satellites, falling around the earth in tight spirals that soon will bring them home. Short-lived and insignificant, they are of our own time and making.

Moonrise, Magnetic Lake

Eternal Forest

The balsam fir are my favorite. I admire their dark, snow-laden boughs along the portage trails. They have full, Christmasy shapes, and their short, flat needles, rolled between your thumb and forefinger, smell fresh and spicy.

The tamaracks live down by the bogs and swamps, their trunks as straight as plumb lines. Many people think they are evergreens, but their lacy, green needles turn dusky amber in fall and leave the trees bare and windblown in winter.

White spruce, tall, full, and broadly cone shaped, grow alone or in small clumps along rivers and lakes. Black spruce, on the other hand, are spindly and huddle shoulder to shoulder in the bogs. All but their uppermost branches may appear dead but are too filled with sap to break for a campfire.

White cedar, too, seek the shoreline and the moist soil of swamps. Their dead lower branches snap off easily and fuel hot, clean fires.

The paper birch are the raw material of bark canoes. Their curls of bark, white outside and buff underneath, burst into hot flame, even when damp. The birch is the harbinger of autumn, its sawtooth leaves turning yellow with the waning days of summer.

Quaking aspen, so named because their fat, spade-shaped leaves shiver in the lightest breeze, grow like weeds in forest openings. Aspen are beaver food. The animals girdle the tree trunks with their chisel teeth and, more by luck than design, drop the trees away from themselves and toward the water, where they strip the tough, juicy bark from the trunks and carry the branches to their lairs and dams.

Red and white pines are kings of the forest, at least in people's minds. Their thick, straight trunks and gigantic spreads of branches and needles so overshadow the other evergreens, literally and figuratively, that someone new to the woods nearly invariably will call any conifer a pine. Pines seek the dry uplands, and a grove of the big trees is the picture of the forest primeval. Their crowns spread above, blocking direct light, and the fallen needles cushion the forest floor, where little underbrush grows because of the constant shade. The largest pines in a stand are all the same age—sometimes three hundred to four hundred years old. They began life together centuries ago, after fire had cleared the land. Some of the giants display scars where subsequent ground fires gnawed away at their tough outer bark. The scars look like cathedral arches, the weathered, gray wood surrounded by a thick lip of gnarled bark.

One hears at times that forests must be logged to stay healthy—pruned and thinned as if they were ornamentals. Forests have lived without logging for millennia and have done so in relative health. Trees need the bite of chain saws and the roar of skidders no more than they need newspapers, furniture, or warm wood stoves. Man needs logging. Trees need fire.

For thousands of years, during the driest days of late summer and autumn, lightning would ignite duff and dead trees, and fire would race across hundreds of square miles. French missionary Father Jean Pierre Aulneau wrote that as he journeyed from Lake Superior to Lake of the Woods he traveled "through fire and a thick, stifling smoke" and failed "even once catching a glimpse of the sun." Hudson's Bay Company trader John D. Cameron observed that "the whole Country almost from one extremity to the other was in a Continual blaze and stopt only by the snows of autumn."

Vulnerable spruces, cedar, and fir usually grow on the wet low ground and the lee side of lakes and cliffs, where the thin-skinned trees stand a good chance of escaping destruction by fire. A crown fire, a conflagration that builds to such intensity it roars from treetop to treetop, nearly clears the land of trees and provides a seedbed for the slow-growing pines. The red and white pines that survive contribute their seeds. The jack pine, a runty species by comparison, grows cones that bristle open at the touch of flame to rain seeds when the fire has passed. Fast-growing birch and aspen, though the parent trees die in the first heat, sprout from old stumps and underground roots to take control of the burn like ground troops. The pines hang back in the shade of the birch and aspen until a light ground fire again sweeps the area, killing the more easily damaged trees and giving the thick-skinned, well-insulated pines light and room to tower over the uplands. Since glacial times it has been like this—fire pushing the patterns of forest across the land like a painter spreading oils across a canvas.

Right– Mixed forest, Mountain Lake
Overleaf– Sunset through Norway-pine needles

A Land Preserved

In a land as old as the Boundary Waters Canoe Area, man's span in time is but a scratch on the bedrock. The recorded history of the region is so brief it is encompassed by the life of a single stand of red pine.

Just off the end of the Gunflint Trail is Threemile Island. About two miles long and a half mile wide, it plugs up the middle of Sea Gull Lake. Much of the island is low and marshy, though several hills, some rising seventy feet above the water, roll across the island like knuckles on a clenched fist. Spread across a small tract is a grove of red pine, tall and straight, each tree bigger around than a person's reach. The Threemile Island pines, about three hundred eighty-five years old, are among the oldest trees—consequently, the oldest living things—in the Boundary Waters Canoe Area. In 1595, when the trees took root in the charred clearing left by a fiercely hot crown fire, the Dakota Indians still lived in canoe country. European explorers, drawn by myth and a glimmer of hope, had just begun to embark from the Eastern Seaboard on long expeditions that would bring them to border country and beyond in a persistent but futile search for the Northwest Passage.

The Ojibway Indians, feeling the push of westward expansion in the eastern Great Lakes region, pushed westward themselves. Migrating along both the north and south shores of Lake Superior, they drove the Dakota from border country onto the plains of Minnesota in the mid-1600s.

In 1660, Pierre Esprit Radisson and Médard Chouart, Sieur des Groseilliers, traveled along the north shore of Lake Superior and may have followed the Pigeon River inland. Jacques de Noyon ascended the Pigeon in 1688 and was the leader of the first European expedition to explore the Boundary Waters. By 1717, according to one French document, the French had "already been clear to the Lake of the Assiniboin"—probably Lake Winnipeg, far northwest of canoe country.

In 1692 a forest fire sweeps Threemile Island, and in 1727 another fire scorches the forest bed, clearing away the undergrowth and fallen trees. The red pines, already more than a century old and three feet around, flourish in the fire's wake and emerge as the dominant trees in their stand. As the burnt land heals, the French build their forts across canoe country, establishing their own dominance and bringing new commerce to the north woods.

Tucked away in a French fur trading post on Lake Superior in 1727 and 1728, Pierre Gaultier, Sieur de la Verendrye, was obsessed by thoughts of a transcontinental route to the Orient. He sought the help of a local Indian, Auchagah, who referred vaguely to the west, where the water tasted bad and moved back and forth. Convinced that the Indian meant the salt water and tides of the Pacific, La Verendrye urged him to draw a map on birch bark. Though Auchagah's drawing bore only the crudest resemblance to an aerial view of the country, it laid out, lake by lake and portage by portage, three routes from Lake Superior to Lake of the Woods, including a course that ran from the mouth of the Pigeon River along what is now the international border. La

Verendrye left with three of his sons in 1731, ascended the Pigeon, and built a post on the Rainy River, the first in a network of forts the French would use in the early days of the fur trade. Auchagah's salty tidal water was probably Hudson Bay, and his map never led La Verendrye to the Pacific. But the map did establish the routes that would be paddled and portaged by the voyageurs, haunted by their songs, and marked by their graves.

French posts began to disappear from the country by 1760, a trend that continued through 1763, when the British won control of Canada. Britain's first major fur company, the Hudson's Bay Company, formed in 1670, gained entry to the interior through Hudson Bay. Several smaller firms sought another route, and in 1768 John Askin began building a fort at Grand Portage near the Pigeon River, the start of the trail through border country. The North West Company, a partnership of Highland Scots formed in 1779, adopted Grand Portage as its inland headquarters.

The era from the late 1700s to the mid-1800s belonged to the voyageurs, the colorful, outrageous, exceedingly durable Canadians who paddled, portaged, and cursed their way across canoe country, transporting furs for the British fur companies.

Most voyageurs came from small farms along the St. Lawrence River near Montreal, where they were engaged for one- to three-year tours in the fur trade. They spoke French and were faithful, if not exemplary, Catholics. Colorfully dressed in deerskin moccasins and leggings, short shirts of buckskin or wool, and tasseled wool caps and sashes, they were small, considerably under six feet, and took little room in a canoe.

Groups of voyageurs set out every spring from Lachine, ascended the Ottawa and Mattawa rivers into Lake Nipissing, sped down the French River to Georgian Bay on Lake Huron, and paddled into and across Lake Superior to Grand Portage with a load of trade goods bound for the interior. After exchanging the load for furs, they returned east. Their bark canoes, thirty-five to forty feet long, were the *canots de maître,* or Montreal canoes. Their diet was salt pork and dried peas or corn, so they were called *mangeurs du lard*—pork eaters.

The men who took trade goods to the interior and returned from the bush to Grand Portage with furs were a different breed of voyageur. They were the *hivernauts*—the winterers. If the *mangeurs du lard* were the apprentices, the *hivernauts* were the journeymen. Paddling twenty-five-foot *canots du nord* over the rugged interior routes through canoe country and as far north as Lake Athabasca, the *hivernauts* began their trip with the hellish Grand Portage. Lugging their packs and 300-pound canoes up a nine-mile portage that rose 760 feet, they by-passed the big falls of the lower Pigeon, including Big Falls, the highest waterfall in Minnesota or along its borders. Despite their size, the voyageurs carried two or three packs at a time—180 to 270 pounds. Legendary *hivernaut* Stephen Bonga boasted that he once carried eight packs. Not surprisingly, a common ailment and occasional killer was strangulated hernia.

The voyageurs' reputation for endurance did not end at water's edge. Once the canoes were loaded, they would pick up their paddles and put them quickly to the water, the paddle strokes beating the rhythm of their songs. They routinely paddled

Right— **Knife Lake**

fifteen to eighteen hours a day. Occasionally two canoes would race side by side for hours. One such race had lasted forty hours when the guides of each party finally ended the contest. Thomas McKenney, who traveled with the voyageurs in 1826, once asked his hard-paddling men if they wished to stop for dinner. "They answered they were fresh yet," he writes. "They had been almost constantly paddling since three o'clock this morning. . . 57,600 strokes of the paddle, and 'fresh yet!' No human beings, except the Canadian French, could stand this." From the morning to 9:30 P.M., when McKenney's voyageurs finally stowed their paddles, they had covered seventy-nine miles.

Their ability to work hard and live freely determined their worth, not only as voyageurs, but as men:

"I could carry, paddle, walk and sing with any man I ever saw," recalled one man more than seventy years old. "I have been twenty-four years a canoeman, and forty-one in service; no portage was ever too long for me. Fifty songs could I sing. I have saved the lives of ten voyageurs, have had twelve wives and six running dogs. I spent all my money on pleasure. Were I young again, I should spend my life the same way over. There is no life so happy as a voyageur's life."

In 1842, the demand for fur waning and the era of the voyageur fading, the United States and Great Britain signed the Webster-Ashburton Treaty, which established the present international boundary through canoe country.

In 1863 and 1864, as the United States struggles with issues of secession and unity, slavery and commerce, a thick, acrid smoke envelops the Threemile Island pines. The biggest fires in centuries consume the tinder-dry forests from the Isabella River north to Saganaga and the forest south of Lac la Croix. Though Threemile Island is spared this conflagration, several hundred square miles, nearly half of the Boundary Waters, burn. The forest will soon recover, however; the fires will prove to have little permanent effect, other than to give life to a younger, more vigorous woods. A greater threat to the land of the Threemile Island pines is on the horizon, and it is coming from the centers of commerce and industry to the south.

The Vermilion gold rush began in 1865, and the area near Vermilion Lake, along the southern fringes of the Boundary Waters, became the infirmary of those infected with gold fever. Some of the best-known men in Minnesota business and politics engaged in the frenzy. It was Minnesota's first taste of gold fever and one of its last. The rush barely survived the year, but it did two things to change forever the fortune of the north woods, which until that time was marked only by the fading trails of the voyageurs and Indians and the rotting forts of the fur trade. First, the rumors of gold spurred the construction of the Vermilion Trail and gave people a way to travel north. Second, the inadvertent—and at the time, seemingly trivial—discovery of iron ore gave people a reason to go north and stay there.

In 1884 the first ore was shipped from the underground iron mines at Tower-Soudan. Townspeople gathered at the tracks and tossed chunks of ore into the railroad cars as the train pulled out of town, bound for loading docks at Two Harbors.

In 1908 the Virginia and Rainy Lake Company opened in the town of Virginia "the largest, most modern and complete lumber plant in the world." By the late 1920s more than a third of the vast stands of virgin timber in what would become the Boundary Waters Canoe Area had been cut over and burned.

By the early 1900s the Threemile Island pines, already in their senescence, have survived to witness a change in the way people think of wilderness. This new philosophy, prompted by an increasing demand for land and resources and a simultaneous desire to preserve what is there, has engendered a controversy that is very much like a fire. As it smolders and periodically bursts into flames, one brigade of political combatants rushes to stoke it, the other hurries to put it out. This may prove to be the most persistent and significant fire of all.

In 1909 President Theodore Roosevelt established Superior National Forest in northeastern Minnesota along the Canadian border.

In the 1920s a controversy over road building led to the designation of roadless "primitive areas" within Superior National Forest.

Proposals for a string of dams from Little Vermilion Lake to Saganaga, as well as other dams outside of the roadless areas, were thwarted in 1930, when Congress passed the Shipstead-Newton-Nolan Act to protect northern Minnesota's waterways from impoundment and its shorelines from logging. The act became a cornerstone for subsequent laws protecting border country. The law carried implications for the rest of the country as well: It was the first statute in which Congress expressly ordered the protection of land as *wilderness*.

Congress reiterated its intentions to protect the wilderness character of Superior National Forest when it passed the Thye-Blatnik Act in 1948. Through this legislation, the Forest Service gained the authority and money to buy private land, particularly resorts, in the roadless areas.

In 1949, by order of President Harry Truman, the planes that fed anglers to fly-in camps were prohibited from flying over the wilderness at less than 4,000 feet.

In 1958 the roadless areas of Superior National Forest were officially named the Boundary Waters Canoe Area.

In 1964 Congress created the federal wilderness system, which included the Boundary Waters Canoe Area. Though many of the legal and philosophical foundations of the wilderness system were laid during the long struggle to preserve canoe country, the Boundary Waters itself was the only area for which exceptions to the law were made. Most notably, logging and motorboats, prohibited elsewhere by the act, still were allowed in much of the Boundary Waters.

In 1978, after a long, simmering, and sometimes explosive controversy over logging, snowmobiles, and motorboats, the region became the Boundary Waters Canoe Area Wilderness. Congress proscribed logging, all but banned snowmobiling, restricted motorboats to about two dozen lakes, and prohibited mining in and near the wilderness.

The Threemile Island pines are now nearly four hundred years old. They have survived the displacement and defeat of a native race, the exploration of a new country, its clearing and excavation for profit, comfort, and adventure, and the beginning of a new awareness that tempers the urge to exploit with an urge to preserve.

The pines, though still tall and solid, soon will die—simply fall one by one of old age, rot, or disease, or burn in an intense fire—and their lives will return to the soil. And when they are gone, what will happen to the land they watched over?

There always will be the familiar calls to turn the land to profit— the trees to pulpwood, the ores to metals. Moreover, new dangers to the wilderness arise continually, the likes of which the nineteenth-century industrialists, the voyageurs, the Ojibway never experienced. Surely one of the most insidious must be acid rain, the invisible fallout of our industrial way of life, which threatens to render lakes in the Boundary Waters lifeless within decades. How can one battle a poison so pervasive?

Unfortunately, the contest over wilderness lands is often tragic; the outcome of the struggle seems to lie in only one direction—toward the demise of wilderness. When the forces of development suffer a setback it is only that—a setback. When the cause of preservation is set back, the result is nearly irrevocable. The parcel of land under contention is lost forever—or, at least, for a good long time. That is why in questions of land use we always must be conservative; we always must err on the side of the land.

Above– **Approaching storm over Loon Lake**
Overleaf– **Red pines**

The Seasons

Spring

Summer

Autumn

Winter

Spring

SPRING HAS TAKEN ME BY SURPRISE THIS YEAR. THREE WEEKS AGO IT WAS SNOWING. SUDDENLY IT IS EARLY MAY, THE LAKES ARE OPEN, SONGBIRDS ARE BUILDING NESTS, THE TEMPERATURE IS EIGHTY DEGREES, AND ALREADY I AM THINKING THAT summer is here. Spring in the Boundary Waters exists less as a season in itself than as simply a transition from winter to summer—a state of mind nurtured by months of deep cold. It is the end of the ice age, and its arrival is tentative and fickle, a race marked by repeated false starts.

On March 21, the vernal equinox, three feet of snow may cover the land, and the temperature may be below zero. By early April the snow will have begun to melt, and the woods will sparkle with the sound of water. Some would call that the beginning of spring. Not me. I know that all thoughts of warmth soon will be buried under a new blanket of snow. I try to withhold my hopes and pronouncements until the turn of the season is irrevocable.

In my mind, there is one sure sign of spring: ice-out. It starts with those same sounds of water. As sun hits the south-facing slopes, snowflakes warm and nestle together. A crystal of ice, sparkling in the light, disappears and seeps into the snowpack. Then another, steeping the ground with fresh meltwater. All across the hills water drips over the outcrops. It moves through the bogs and into the lakes. The nearly inaudible trickle in the high ground becomes the steady roar of water in the river. At the same time, the snow on the lakes settles until it melts to slush. The ice becomes gray and soft—people up here call it "punky" or "rotten." It melts around the edges of the lake and drifts from shore to shore, breaking and piling up on the beach. After a few sunny days or a warm, heavy rain, with startling swiftness it is gone.

Spring, finally, is here.

Warmth and sun, new leaves and signs of life—that was last week. This week a chill wind blows, and snowflakes swirl to the ground. It is as though the calendar is turning backwards.

Spring makes canoeing possible once again. The rivers are high, and though the high water creates some powerful and dangerous rapids, it also floats canoes through shallows that later will be impassable. Spring can pose problems on the portages, however. Rain and the thawing of the ground can turn a trail into a soft, quivering mass of mud.

When I was a Boy Scout many years ago, I took a long trip through the Boundary Waters and northward into the Quetico region of Ontario. Groups of scouts were led by guides who paddled long, graceful wood-and-canvas canoes. Though the rest of us made do with aluminum canoes, we were taught to treat our boats as if they were made of the more fragile canvas. We were exhorted *never* to let our canoes touch the rocks; so as we approached shore, we jumped into the lake—thigh deep in some cases—lifted the boats from the water, and swung them onto our shoulders. They were heavy-gauge aluminum, but tradition, not common sense, dictated our treatment of them.

The guide for my group weighed little more than his precious wood-and-canvas canoe once it had soaked up several pounds of water in the course of a trip. But he was powerfully built—he was a wrestler for one of the big midwestern universities, as I recall—and whenever we reached a portage, he threw his pack up onto his back, waded into the lake, shouldered the canoe, and trotted down the trail, carrying everything in one trip.

For several days we scouts talked of a particular portage we soon would make. It was nearly two miles long, and we viewed each portage as preparation for *the* portage. Finally the moment arrived.

Our guide, as usual, shouldered his boat, shot down the trail, and soon was out of sight. We struggled with our canoes, making sure neither to drag them on the rocks nor hit them on the trees lining the path. After a half-hour we knew we were much nearer exhaustion than the end of the portage. To make matters worse, the trail was becoming wetter and harder to follow. Nothing tests your resolve like the thought that you might be lost. Finally, however, we found our guide. Trudging around a bend, we discovered him mired to his hips in mud and sinking. With one loud curse he lifted his sleek, hand-crafted canoe and sent it sailing from his shoulders. It bounced off a tree, caromed off a rock, rolled, and came to rest in the muck.

Rules, I gathered, are made to be broken.

Left– Ice breakup, Seagull Lake
Overleaf– Water smartweed, Granite River

The Resurgence of Life

Spring is a time of new sounds, forgotten during the winter, and new evidence of life that was covered by the snow and suppressed by the cold, and there is no better place to look for it than at a beaver pond.

This particular pond is along the portage route into Angleworm Lake near the Echo Trail. The time is early May. Ice still clings to a few north-facing cliffs, and in the deep shade beneath a stand of spruce a patch of dirty snow lies by a little brook. Nevertheless, the day is warm, and the woods are filled with noises and movement. Small, quick warblers and sparrows flit close to the ground, gathering sticks and wisps of grasses for their nests. A pair of hairy woodpeckers pick at tree trunks in search of insects, and yellow-shafted flickers fly down the trail in their bouncing, uneven fashion, rising and falling in their paths of flight like roller coasters. We are at first puzzled by a high-pitched drone in a stand of black spruce but then realize it is the buzzing of flies in the dense branches.

As we walk within sight of the pond, a flock of mallards jumps from the water into the air. Quacking with surprise, they fly down river and out of sight. Our trail crosses a little creek right in front of the beaver dam, a four-foot-high thatchwork of branches and mud. Water spills over the dam and races across an outcrop on the trail into another pond. The dam has raised the level of water behind it at least three feet, drowning and killing the trees that stood next to what once was a marshy little stream. The beavers—or several successive beaver families—must have maintained this dam for several decades, for the dead trees now tower above the water, their trunks weathered and dry, smooth except for a few gray branches that reach out like the bleached bones of a skeleton in a house of horrors. Another sign that the beaver have been here a long time is the absence of aspen, their staple, along shore. Only at the far end of the pond is there a small pocket of the trees—and they are one hundred to two hundred feet from the water, a dangerous situation for the beaver. After the animals fell and eat the aspen next to their ponds, they face two choices: move to another stretch of river or wander far-

ther ashore for food. Either choice spells the end of beaver in the area, at least until the aspen grow back. If they stray too far in search of aspen, the beaver, slow and clumsy on land, are easy prey for wolves. By regularly moving their dams upstream or downstream, the beaver create new openings in the forest, places of life where two kinds of habitat touch—in this case, the forest and the marsh—to the benefit of animals in both.

This broad, shallow, nearly stagnant pond was probably one of the first bodies of water to open this spring. Though the big, deep lakes are still cold, the water here has warmed and is coming to life. Red-winged blackbirds lurk in the reeds and cattails. Grackles and tree swallows perch on the branches of the old, dead trees. Water striders speed across the pond's surface, their light, spiderlike bodies supported by the surface tension. Whirligig beetles spin their quick, tight arcs across the water, traveling from here to there as though they were waltzers tracing big circles across the dance floor.

We leave the beaver pond for a while and follow an irregular, lackadaisical course, first up one side of Angleworm Lake and then the other. The lake itself is narrow, some three miles long and a quarter-mile wide, flanked on each side by cliffs and overlooks. We hike up the east side of the lake, where the trail takes off along a ridge that follows a little stream into a deep valley. We rest on a granite dome that overlooks the creek far below and a rolling sea of pine-covered hills in the distance. Birch and aspen are beginning to leaf out and make broad swaths of light green amid the darker conifers. As the shadows of the hills stretch farther over the valley, we reluctantly decide to head back.

We retrace our steps to the beaver pond, sit on the outcrop by the dam, and savor the scene a final time. When the sun hits only the treetops and the sky turns red, the frogs begin to sing. A few sporadic, deep croaks punctuate a series of cricketlike chirps that, when multiplied by the thousands, fill the pond with a barrage of frog song.

Early-arriving loon
Right– Spring foliage, Rose Lake

Above– Evening grosbeak
Below– Mud turtle

Right– Loon Lake
Overleaf– Basswood River

Above– **Otter, Rat Lake**
Below– **Young mergansers, South Arm of Knife Lake**

Left– **Looking west over Rose Lake**

33

Summer

SUMMER—SO LONG IN COMING, SO SHORT IN DURATION. SLOWLY AND GRADUALLY, LIKE THE ONSET OF BLISSFUL DREAMING, THE WARMING WEATHER NUDGES THE FOREST TOWARD THE LUSH FULL FLUSH OF LIFE AND INDOLENCE. THE trees and shrubs show thick, green foliage. The frenzy of spring migration and mating finished, fish move to their usual depths, and birds tend to their nests and young. Mosquitoes swarm, black flies bite, and no-see-ums, gnatlike but as small as grains of sand, leave mysterious pinpricks of blood. Canoeists paddle the waters, carry pack and canoe down portages, and explore the small lakes, streams, and beaver ponds off the main routes. It is easy to lose ambition for a fast-paced trip and, instead, lounge on a big outcrop, dive into the cool water, crawl back onto warm rock, and sleep in the sun.

Strawberries ripen in June or early July. Wild strawberries are small—not much larger than peas. Even in a good patch they are scattered and generally not worth the trouble it takes to pick them. Juneberries and raspberries ripen a month later. They often are plentiful and easy to pick, but they still aren't worth my time, because to pick them would keep me from blueberries, the best of northern Minnesota fruits.

Blueberry picking provokes a fervor that supersedes common sense. I read recently about a seventy-six-year-old man whose zeal for finding ever-richer patches of blueberries led him into the wilds near Crane Lake, on the western tip of the Boundary Waters. The woods are thick, the roads few, the lakes and rivers a bewildering maze. A person wandering into such wilderness conceivably might not be rescued for years, but this man was lucky. He was found two days later—eating blueberries, presumably.

A few years ago a woman picking berries lost her way near Ely. "She just went out for the day," said a fellow who works for the U.S. Forest Service there. "She got turned around in a swamp. That's where they saw her from the airplane—up to her waist in muck." Getting lost or stranded is not the only berry-picking hazard, however. Insects are another. Horse flies and deer flies painfully extract tiny pieces of human flesh. A friend of mine says his earliest recollection of berry picking is that of being covered with ants.

Sometimes the pests are larger. Bears like blueberries, too. I figure they need them more than I do, and if I were to meet a bear in a berry patch, I probably would yield to it on that principle. A few summers ago, a woman went afield, her dachshund running ahead to frolic in the blueberry patch. Deeply absorbed in her berry picking, the woman suddenly was startled by the sound of thrashing brush. She looked up in time to see a wolf tackle her dog about thirty feet away, shake it, and drag it into the woods.

All that for a few pints of berries. But I know how it feels. Once I set my bucket in the midst of a patch, my enthusiasm is ignited; if there are really big blueberries about, I can continue picking for hours.

One muggy summer day, after nearly three hours of scrambling through brush and poison ivy, and picking, shaking, and raking blueberries into aluminum cookpots, my wife and I were driving back to the Twin Cities. Cynthia started from her sleep in the passenger seat. "Every time I close my eyes," she said, "I see blueberries."

We switched places in Eveleth and resumed the long drive home. She was right. I closed my eyes and blueberries appeared —ripe ones as big as marbles, smothered with powdery, frosty gloss. They fell into the bucket from their own weight and hit the bottom with the sound of steady rain. Glistening acres of berries lay before my eyes, as bright and thick as poppies in Flanders fields—a vision of the ultimate blueberry patch.

Left– **Kekekabic Lake**
Overleaf– **Sunrise on Knife Lake**

Devil's Elbow, Granite River

39

Lady Boot Bay

Above– **Lac la Croix**
Below– **Granite River**

40

Thomas Lake

Above– **Fireweed**
Below right– **Blueberry blossoms**
Below left– **Water lily**

Thimbleberry
Overleaf– Lower Basswood Falls

43

Thunderstorm, Loon Lake

Beginning of Lower Basswood Falls

Brule Lake

Above– **Ester Lake**
Below– **Isabella River**

Overleaf– **Knife Lake**

Boulder Lake campsite

The Circle of Light

Some campfires are good for light, some for heat. Some are good for neither, leaving your clothes smelling like smoked fish, your eyelids red and swollen, and your corneas like sun-baked mud. This campfire, however, is good for both. The cedar sticks—all broken by hand, for I rarely carry a hatchet—burn hot, bright, and clean. The wood crackles, snaps, and sizzles, and the fire lights a little circle of woods as it roasts our faces. We quietly watch the flames until one of my companions says, "Looking into a fire—I wonder whether it extends to earlier roots somewhere."

I have thought about that often. Why build a fire and sit around it for hours? Perhaps because it animates the darkness—the only actor on an otherwise dark stage. But I think there is another, better reason, and it has to do less with the fire at our faces than with the woods at our backs. In the dark woods the fire is our last retreat.

I recall a trip down the Granite River, when we set camp in deep woods and brush overlooking Gneiss Lake. It had been a long day but not a particularly challenging one, and we were feeling indolent as well as tired. When the canoes were put away and dinner done, the pink twilight showed no signs of rain; so while the others sat around the fire, I carried my sleeping bag down to shore, where I planned to sleep under the stars. I tramped out a level spot near the lake. Darkness was gathering, the woods were quiet, and the water still.

Something big jumped. So did I.

A black bear clutched a pine tree ten feet away. I yelled and it shinned up the tree.

"Really?" Wayne asked when I told the others about the bear. Wayne—small, scrappy, built of sinew and muscle—is a profound skeptic but is willing to entertain even the most improbable tale for a few minutes. He considered my report for about three seconds and began to laugh. So did everyone else.

"I'm not kidding. Go look."

We hiked down to shore. The bear, now ten feet up the tree, was swatting our food pack.

"Get out of there!" Wayne yelled, and the bear climbed a few feet higher. As black bears go, it was big—three hundred pounds perhaps. Its legs hugging the tree and claws gripping the bark, it opened its big, pink mouth and hissed. It was a sound I'd never heard, and I don't know how else to describe it. It was a loud, nasal, frightening hiss.

Knowing there was no use in keeping the bear treed, we climbed back up the bluff to the fire and waited several minutes. Black bears are pests but are rarely aggressive. We were sure this one would climb down and make its escape in the gathering darkness.

But when we returned to shore, the bear was sitting next to the tree trunk. We began to shout and bang pots. Wayne threw a stick. The bear didn't run as I expected but turned and slowly walked. Heavy fat rippled under its skin. It stopped and looked at us, hissed once more, and then ambled away. I felt we had not seen the last of it.

Back at camp, we encircled the fire and the fire encircled us—eight people and a dog. The dog, a German shepherd, had shown scant interest in the bear at first, but as we had driven the bear from its tree, the dog began to bark and lunge against its tightly held collar. Now, however, it lay at our feet, intercepting some of the fire's heat and light, as we told stories. I realized our voices were louder than normal, our laughter more forced. Occasionally the dog sat up, cocked its ears, and looked to the woods as if something dwelt outside the reach of firelight.

The crack of a branch behind me was loud and startling, though its cause was no mystery. The dog began to cry and howl. We raced into the darkness. The bear's black coat soaked up the beam of the flashlight. We shouted and threw sticks, rocks, anything, trying to drive the bear off without enraging it. Its eyes flecks of light, it gums and tongue hot and fleshy, the bear hissed, then walked without haste into the forest.

We made plans in the light of the fire and dashed into the darkness to execute them. We dropped our food packs from the tree near shore and brought them to the fire. We gathered more wood, briefly leaving the security of the firelight to grope in the dark woods. Finally, we talked of leaving. I argued that we'd get no sleep while the bear prowled. Wayne hated to relinquish the campsite to the bear or to acknowledge his fear. Perhaps he had none.

"I think the best thing is to get some sleep," Wayne said. "That bear isn't going to do anything. I'm going to bed."

Wayne dragged his sleeping bag and ground cloth from his pack and stretched out just beyond the firelight. I wasn't sure whether his determination was encouraging or shaming, but I too began to think of sleep. Not right now—the fire was too comforting—but soon.

"Aaauughh!"

We ran to Wayne. He was curled into a little ball inside his sleeping bag.

"He almost stepped on me."

Our flashlight caught the bear as it slipped into the brush less than twenty feet away. Wayne and his sleeping bag returned to the fire.

We began taking down tents and stuffing packs. The canoes, unfortunately, were down the shore 200 feet, beyond an obstacle course of rocks, brush, and trees. In the dark it would be difficult to move all the gear down there, and once we reached the boats and paddled onto the lake, it would be too dark to find another camp. We decided to wait by the campfire until the moon rose.

We stoked the fire for bright flames, though we were careful not to burn all our wood and be forced to scavenge more. The fire dimmed as a new stick absorbed its heat, flared as it caught, and dimmed again as the wood fell into ashes. The flames danced and cast leaping shadows in a little circle of light that defined our territory in the nighttime woods. The effect of firelight in the forest is a strange one: All around is the brightness and the glow of tree trunks, then, suddenly, blackness, as though the light had cooled and fallen to earth. We embraced the fire—for hours, it seemed. The occasional snap of a twig warned us that the bear was stalking us just beyond the reach of light. When the moon finally cleared the trees, we lifted our packs. After one last look for anything we might have forgotten, we doused the flames and made our way through the dark for the canoes.

Without the light of the fire, our eyes adjusted quickly to the luminescent sky over the lake. A half-mile away was a small island, a hump of rock covered by a few short trees and scrubby bushes. We paddled toward it and landed. Only a few yards wide and thirty yards long, it was too small to conceal any bears. All around us the lake lay like a protective moat. We immediately fell to sleep; there was no need for a fire.

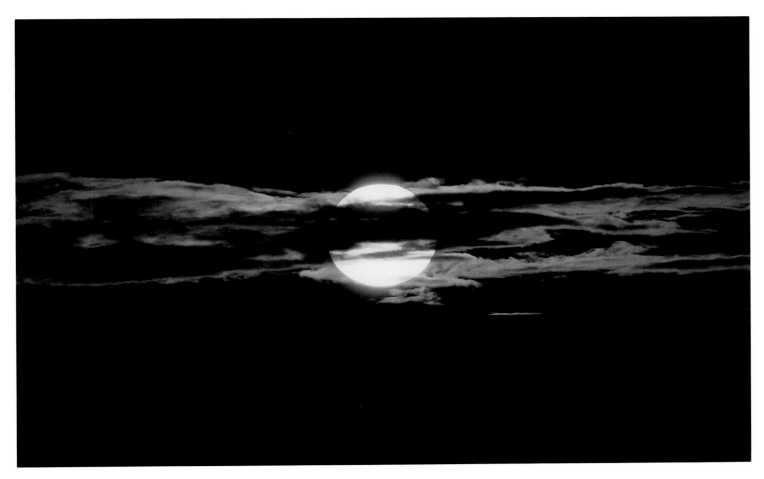

Moonrise, Gillis Lake

Looking east toward Rove Lake

Near the pictographs on Basswood River

55

The differences that distinguish the tacky from the quaint and the commonplace from the mysterious are sometimes subtle. Compare, for example, an abandoned, dilapidated mining settlement with a mobile home court. One is charming and interesting; the other, noisy and desperate. To hike through the woods and unexpectedly find the first is exciting; to discover the second, dismaying. The old mining houses and the trailer homes are similar products of different ages. Both are cheap housing, built quickly with little attention given to aesthetics. Yet one seems appealing—"historic," and the other seems to exist on the tattered edge of middle-class dreams, slipping rapidly toward squalor. Like the residents of the trailers, the old-time miners and their families may have felt the reins on life slipping from their hands. But the gauze of time diffuses the misery, and the town's abandonment gives it romance.

I mention this to try to explain the appeal of the Indian pictographs, those haunting, nearly indelible renderings of birds, animals, men, and demigods. Some of the drawings are crude and wooden. Others are graceful and surprisingly detailed. Some are realistic, others grotesque. All are intriguing. But why, after all, are they different from "Class of '64" scrawled on an underpass? There are, I think, three reasons: They are old, we don't know what they mean, and their makers are long dead.

Nearly three hundred pictographs have been documented at sites scattered across Canada, from the Great Lakes, to Hudson Bay, to the Northwest Territories. There are several pictographs in the Boundary Waters as well, including the well-known paintings on Crooked Lake below Basswood Falls and two groups on Lac la Croix. But few are as distinct or as tightly composed as those on North Hegman Lake. The brick-red pictures cover a flat, pink span between the fissures on a twenty-foot overhanging cliff. A scarecrow of a man stands about a foot high, long arms outstretched and fingers spread. Directly beneath him is a dog, perhaps a wolf. To the right is a moose with large antlers, a pronounced bell, and splayed hooves. Next to the man's head are six or seven horizontal marks. Above him are three crescent lines—apparently canoes. Two canoes carry two men each, one is empty. Above this tightly composed group is a big, red X.

An Ojibway, perhaps a *miday*—a member of the Grand Medicine Society—once scrambled from a canoe onto the ledge that runs along the cliff about eight feet above the lake. He reached into a birch-bark or pottery vessel full of red ocher and made a paste, mixing the ocher with sturgeon or whitefish oil, animal fat, egg, or glue rendered from fish or animals. He then smeared the mixture onto the cliff, using two or three fingers for the bodies of the creatures and a single finger for the fine lines of the man's hands, the moose's hooves, and the canoes. The binder dried and leached out in time, leaving the powder bound to the microscopic irregularities of the cliff. The pigment demonstrates incredible persistence, as James Isham noted in his *Observations* in the 1740s: "The Glue the Natives saves out of the Sturgeon is Very strong and good, they use itt in mixing with their paint, which fixes the Colours so they never Rub out."

Explorers and modern travelers alike have puzzled over the ages of the pictographs. Some paintings, described in journals nearly two centuries ago, are still legible. Others depict guns and

other fur trade goods and clearly were painted after the arrival of Europeans. But the ages of most, including the North Hegman Lake pictographs, remain a complete mystery.

Their meanings are just as much in doubt. Time seems to have robbed the Ojibways themselves of the art of interpreting the paintings. Nonetheless, they appear to express the mysticism the Ojibways developed in response to the wilderness around them. Geologist Joseph G. Norwood concluded that the paintings marked holy places. He wrote in 1849: "At a point, called by the Indians *Wa-bi-se-gon,* near the entrance to Nemakan or Sturgeon Lake, is an exposure of mica slate, with felspar veins... which, from the resemblance of one of the veins to a serpent, is regarded by the Indians as a manitou or god, and must be highly esteemed by them, from the quantity of vermilion bestowed on it, and the number of animals depicted on the face of the rock."

"To all appearances, the aboriginal artist was groping toward the expression of the magical aspect of his life, rather than taking pleasure in the world of form around him," writes Selwyn Dewdney, who chased across much of Canada and northern Minnesota, searching out pictographs for his book *Indian Rock Paintings of the Great Lakes,* first published in 1962. The most curious renderings Dewdney examined were of *maymaygwayshi,* legendary imps said to live underwater or in rocky fissures along lakes and streams. Fond of upsetting canoes or stealing fish from nets, *maymaygwayshi* are ashamed of their faces because, according to various legends, they have beards or lack the fleshy parts of their noses.

Dewdney himself wasn't always sure whether *maymaygwayshi* were depicted on the rocks or were themselves the artists. One man told Dewdney that a human form painted in a surrender pose was a *maymaygwayshi,* though another said the mysterious fairies reached above water to leave their own red hand prints on the cliffs. Another Ojibway told Dewdney about two boys who disappeared. A few days after their disappearance, the sorrowful father was fishing when he saw red paintings on a cliff. "So then he thought the boys was in the rocks there," the Indian told Dewdney. "They stole the boys—*maymaygwayshiwuk* did—canoe and everything."

Miday, Dewdney was told, used their powers to pierce the painted cliffs and trade tobacco and clothing for "rock medicine" from the *maymaygwayshi.* In fact, the practice of leaving gifts persists. Dewdney once searched a ledge for offerings to the *maymaygwayshi* and found a cellophane-wrapped cigar.

Dewdney never did interpret the pictographs. He simply had no reasonable evidence from which to draw a conclusion. Others haven't shown so much restraint. That something could be inscrutable is too much for most of us to bear, and we fill the gap with fables. Before my own trip to the North Hegman Lake pictographs, I read a description of the paintings based on an old newspaper account. The story said the pictures "marked the meeting place of two Indian parties. One party came, waited, and finally left the drawings as a message for the other party. Near the top of the picture are three canoes... that indicate the size of the party. The canoes all point north, indicating the direction the party took when it left. Below the canoes are seven marks, indicating that seven fires were built (this means seven days were

Left– **Pictographs on Basswood River**
Right– **Close-up of bird and canoe, Basswood River pictographs**

spent waiting for the second party to arrive). The large man represents an Indian who killed the moose with the gigantic set of horns and the wolf. The line below them indicates that the animal carcasses were taken with the party, since it points north also. Since the man is 10 inches to 12 inches high, the Indians were probably not just an ordinary hunting party. The berry juices used as paints remain clear and legible.''

As I stood at the base of the cliff, I remembered this story

and tried to imagine the planned meeting of two hunting parties. Strain as I might, however, I couldn't tell which way the canoes were headed. Moreover, the paintings clearly were not made with berry juices. It seemed the newspaper scribe turned to his imagination when his understanding gave out, perhaps much as the Ojibway themselves had done through their painted rocks and *maymaygwayshi.*

Autumn

WHEN THE WILD RICE RIPENED, SPREADING PURPLE SWATHS ACROSS THE LAKESHORES AND MARSHY RIVERSIDES, THE OJIBWAY KNEW AUTUMN WAS COMING. NOWADAYS WE ARE BETTER ACQUAINTED WITH THE TIME clock and calendar than with the seasons and fruits of the land, and we might put it the other way: It's late August; the rice will be ready soon (provided, of course, we are even dimly aware of what wild ricing is). The native grain was a staple of the Indians. Now it has become something of a delicacy, selling for more than two dollars a pound raw and up to ten dollars processed. Many ricers, in fact, can scarcely afford to eat it; a pound is worth three loaves of Wonderbread.

Ricing begins when the kernels darken and pop easily from the plant. The rice is gathered in canoes, the sternman standing, propelling the boat through the rice beds with a duck-billed pole. The beater, sitting amidships, swings two eighteen-inch sticks, one in each hand. The first swishing stroke brings the heads of rice over the gunwale. The second knocks the grain into the bottom of the canoe. What is missed will feed the ducks and sow next year's crop. The movement is rhythmic, methodical, almost mechanical, and the sound of wood striking rice has been heard on the waning days of summer for centuries.

The birch turn first. As the days grow shorter, the other trees soon follow, bursting into their resplendence.

Whitefish, schooling by the hundreds, congregate in the shallows of lakes and swim up shallow, quiet tributary streams.

The white-tailed deer enter their rut. The bucks' antlers shed their velvet and turn sleek and glossy. The males expend their aggressiveness in clashes with saplings and other bucks, and in the yearly ritual of mating.

Birds gather in flocks, some species preparing for migration south. Others begin arriving from their summering grounds to the north.

Everywhere animals are moving, storing food. The red squirrel gathers pine cone seeds, and the black bear forages, building up layers of fat to carry it through long months of winter dormancy.

The fish, birds, and animals have a sense—an instinctive urge to prepare for something, without knowing or remembering what is in store for them.

In the morning we slide the canoe into the water. The shade protects the frost on the leaves and stones near shore. We paddle down a little creek. I hear a faint tinkle near shore that follows us down river. We look, see nothing, and paddle on, but still we hear it. It sounds like the touch of wind chimes. We pivot the canoe, sweep past the marsh grass, and once again investigate. Then we see it—ice. A fragile sheet left by the night was broken by the wave from our canoe. Thin and clear like mica, it distorts the sand and pebbles in the creek bed. A gentle touch breaks off a big piece and sets it adrift, invisible on the water.

The rest of the days are warm and sunny, and we see no more ice. Nonetheless, its first appearance was a melancholy omen. As I watch the warm days fade, I regret that I've failed to make the most of them, to seize each moment. As surely as the ice will take hold at water's edge and slowly crawl across entire lakes, sealing them shut for the winter, time is taking hold of my life and foreclosing any chance that I can reclaim what I once let slip by. Preoccupied by the past—all the things left unsaid, things put aside until later—I also am consumed by the future, and like the animals, I feel a dull urge to prepare for something.

Left– **Little Indian Sioux River**
Overleaf– **Fairy ring**

Ensign Lake

63

Alice Lake

Aerial view near Basswood Lake

Approaching fall storm, Jackfish Bay
Overleaf– Saganaga Lake

End of a portage trail

Jack pine

Maple leaves

Friday Bay, Crooked Lake

Little Saganaga Lake

Evening paddle, Parent Lake
Overleaf– **Northern lights**

Portage trail, Vera Lake

Dorothy's fence, compliments of visitors

Lives Apart

I once met a man who had taken to the Boundary Waters to learn more about society by living without it for awhile—a modern-day Thoreau. In his thirties, he was small and sinewy, and he cropped his dark hair close to the scalp with a hunting knife. Spending his days in isolation, he would summer in a tent and winter in a wigwam of plastic sheeting and blankets, heated by a wood stove made from a turpentine can. He made his shoes from deer hide and padded his bed with cedar needles. He ate beans, rice, wild plants, and what game and fish he could catch. He would travel—by canoe in summer, on showshoes in winter—to Ely and spend about two hundred fifty dollars a year for food and goods. He made me promise to keep his name and many details of his life a secret. Few people know about this elusive character, and for that matter, I don't know myself whether he still lives there.

He was one of only three people to make a permanent home in the Boundary Waters in recent years. The other two, Benny Ambrose and Dorothy Molter, were better known—Dorothy is nearly famous. Until Benny's death of a heart attack in August 1982, he and Dorothy were neighbors in the frontier sense of the word. Some years they saw each other once or twice, some years not at all. When canoeists stopped to talk to Benny, he would load them up with rutabagas, carrots, and potatoes to carry down to Dorothy.

Benny came north from Iowa after World War I to prospect for gold. He then ricocheted around northern Minnesota and much of Canada and lived for many years in a tiny, one-room log cabin on Cypress Lake. He made more money by guiding, trapping, and running a drill rig for someone else than he did by prospecting for himself. Benny was married many years back and raised two daughters. He dismissed the divorce simply: "She wanted me to leave the woods, but that's out." He cultivated a small garden next to his house, fortifying the thin soils of the Canadian Shield with rich Iowa dirt and with muck shoveled from beaver dams. Benny, fiery and outspoken, didn't mind visitors—as long as they didn't linger. "Got no time for it," he

would say. "I've got work to do."

While Benny shunned attention, Dorothy Molter has grown used to it. A 1952 *Saturday Evening Post* story called Dorothy the "loneliest woman in America," a description that may be accurate during border country winters but belies the attention she gets in the summer, when droves of canoes drift past her cabin on Knife Lake. She keeps a log of visitors and some years tallies more than seven thousand. She is so well known around northern Minnesota that she has received letters addressed: Dorothy, Ely, Minnesota.

Over the years Dorothy has also been called the Florence Nightingale of the north woods. A registered nurse, she has snowshoed for miles in sub-zero weather to treat others when rough ice prevented ski planes from delivering doctors. A camper once stumbled and somehow planted the back of his head on an axe. Dorothy shaved the wound and closed it with adhesive tape. A Minneapolis woman once tried suicide with an overdose of barbiturates, and Dorothy kept her alive with cold packs, strong coffee, enemas, and constant walks. When a boy gashed his foot, Dorothy disinfected the cut and, with the help of a visiting dentist, sewed the wound shut. There was no anesthesia; so Dorothy, the dentist, the boy's father, and a friend had to pin the screaming patient to the kitchen table during the operation.

"I didn't come up here to get away from people," Dorothy says.

Set in a tall virgin stand of red pine, Dorothy's place was once a resort called the Isle of Pines. Her home is scattered across a cluster of three islands interconnected by wooden footbridges. Her summer tent is on one island, where she has a sweeping view of Knife Lake. When Jerry Stebbins and I visited in October 1978, Dorothy was not to be found. The tent was tied shut. We paddled over to the main island, where her winter cabin faces a protected bay. Her yard exemplified entrenched wilderness landscaping. There were old sleds, boats, a snowmobile, a ladder, shovels, a scythe, buckets, stovepipes, a

Dorothy Molter

Winter

I N THE SILENT, WHITE BLANKET OF WINTERTIME, TRACKS TELL THE STORY. TWO PARALLEL TRACKS, NOW HARD AND CRUSTED, MARK THE ROUTE A SKIER TOOK OVER A LAKE SEVERAL DAYS EARLIER. UP ON SHORE, IN A THICKET OF ASPEN SAPLINGS, A HOLE IN THE FLUFFY snow, edged with the whisper of wing tips, shows where a ruffed grouse burrowed to survive a cold night. The tracks of the snowshoe hare are frequent in this country; when the hare runs it leaves a telltale and familiar impression—two big rear-paw prints well spaced and in the lead, and the small front-foot tracks close together behind them. The arrangement looks peculiar, backwards, until one realizes that the hare stretched forward with its front legs before springing and stamping its rear feet nearly into the same tracks as it bounded away in a snowstorm of speed. Like the hare, the Canada lynx has feet enlarged by bristly fur. The big cat can chase across the snow as quickly as the rabbit and, if it has the advantage of surprise, strike down its favorite prey.

Red-backed voles, deer mice, and masked shrews tunnel beneath the snow, finding refuge from predators and the cold. After each new snow a hard crust forms over the burrows, keeping the rodents safe from all but the tube-shaped weasel, which also can squeeze into the tunnels. Where a foot trail breaches this maze, a mouse may leap into the sunlight for one vulnerable second—an elusive target for an owl or red fox—dash across the dazzling snow, and dive once again into the safety of its winter lair.

Ravens, sentries of the woods, attend a scene of death. Glistening black and as smug as cats, they squawk, flap, and drift from treetop to treetop, always watching. As I trudge through the snow they soar off. Some of them, reluctant to abandon their find, move to trees only a couple of hundred feet away. Deer hair is strewn in the blood-spattered snow. Only the skull and biggest bones are left, covered with blood and sinew. Hide-covered lower legs, hooves attached, lie in the snow, bent as if frozen in mid-leap. A circle of snow around the kill is trampled hard with wolf prints. Were I a better tracker and more patient, I could follow the tracks backwards to learn how it happened—the pack catching the deer's scent, the surprised deer discovering the danger too late, an explosion of powdery snow, the deer quickly falling as the wolves rip its flanks and legs. Studied with diligence, the tracks will tell all of this. But the trails sneak under a tangle of brush and lead far up a ridge, and I soon give up and content myself with what I can imagine.

Maybe the ravens know.

Unless one has vast experience with north country winters, it is nearly impossible to recall the intensity of cold on a night in January in the Boundary Waters. I have spent my share of time in the outdoors in that time of year, but even so, I have not lived in it from day to day. Sitting here in my warm home, I find it difficult to imagine the full impact of winter's continuous and unrelenting cold. My own inability to do this reminds me of the protagonist in Jack London's "To Build a Fire," a man killed by his refusal to recognize the danger of winter and his failure "to meditate upon his frailty as a creature of temperature, and upon man's frailty in general, able only to live within certain narrow limits of heat and cold." In winter, cold rules, it dominates, it suppresses, and what it must be like to live in it most of us will never understand.

Left– **Sawbill Lake**
Overleaf– **Stairway Portage**

Winter Camping

Winter campsite, twenty-five degrees below zero and falling

The cold descended like mist, creeping in around my parka hood and settling on my shoulders. It seemed that my breath would freeze and fall to the snow. The black sky was as clear as a diamond, the starlight so bright it appeared to crackle on the crisp air. The sharp night cold robbed the fire of everything but its light, and the gas flame of a cookstove had little more effect than the beam of a flashlight. We had no thermometer but guessed the temperature to be thirty degrees below zero and falling when we went to bed. Heavy snow lay thigh deep around my tent, which was zipped tight except for two small openings at each end to let out the wet air of breathing. Two foam pads fended off the snow's cold, and two sleeping bags kept away the cold air. I was wearing two sweaters, wool pants, two pairs of wool socks, and a ski mask. The hoods of the sleeping bags were pulled tight around my face, and I was sure I would die, freeze without the chance to awake in panic.

I didn't die, of course—didn't even come close. On the contrary, I woke up in the morning in a mad sweat. In the winter, there is such a thin line between comfort and discomfort that you can lie in your sleeping bag, sticky under the arms yet feeling a fleeting shiver, like the passing of a shadow. You are sure that if the temperature drops a single degree, you'll fall into convulsions, your teeth chattering and bones rattling. I had been so worried about getting cold that I had overdressed, and in the morning my sleeping bag was soaked with moisture and caked with frost. No, unless you freeze a finger or toe, or break through thin ice, winter's cold isn't nearly so aggravating as winter's dark-

ness. The sun sets at five in the afternoon and rises at eight in the morning—fifteen hours of darkness. What human being could sleep fifteen hours a day? Winter's major challenge is not staying warm, but keeping occupied when it is too dark to wander off through the woods. We sit in the firelight for hours, gathering wood smoke, considering it a moral and practical victory if we can forestall bedtime until nine. Then, having been careful not to drink too much beforehand, we climb into our tents and prepare to lie still until sunup, eleven hours away.

Why contrive ways to defeat the darkness and cold and be content to only half succeed? Some people have no choice. Ensconced in homesteads at the fringes of the wilderness, they run trap lines or cut pulp, and enduring winter is a matter of survival. Then there are people like me, city dwellers who could stay warmly tucked inside houses and offices all winter except that we would begin to act irritably and irrationally about February. In a region where frost can nip the leaves in late August and linger until early June, one must learn to enjoy the winter. That too is a matter of survival. Besides, the intense cold and interminable darkness aside, winter has a few things to say for itself. Crisp mornings as clear as crystal. Glistening, frost-covered trees— cathedrals of ice and sunlight in the woods. The contrast of a running stream set amid snow fields and frozen lakes. Quiet snows in March, the big, juicy flakes falling as softly as clouds touching. With the traveling hordes of summer safe in their homes, winter belongs to the wilderness.

White-tailed deer

Brule Lake

Cedars along Hungry Jack Lake

Ice crystals

91

Above– Duncan Lake
Overleaf– West Bearskin Lake

Epilogue

ONCE STUMBLED ACROSS A QUOTE BY GERTRUDE STEIN THAT TO ME EXPLAINS NOT ONLY THE IMPRINT THAT WILDERNESS LEFT ON THE AMERICAN CHARACTER, BUT ALSO THE ORIGINS OF OUR FEELINGS TOWARD WILD LAND:

"In the United States there is more space where nobody is than where anybody is.

"This is what makes America what it is."

Many of the stereotypes we hold dear—self-reliance, ingenuity, perseverance, even downright obstinacy—arise from the image of our forebears hacking a path of civilization across the wild continent. To them, the frontier was the battle line advanced against wilderness. Beyond the frontier lay a vast, lawless land. Though a few people, mainly Indians and enemies of the new nation, found freedom there, most of our ancestors feared it and tried as hard as they could to destroy it. To a great degree they succeeded. The frontier retreated before their westward march until, sometime near the turn of the century, it fell into the Pacific. We have been looking for a frontier ever since. Even today, a good many of us think of woodsmanship as a birthright. Throw someone from the city into the wilderness, and immediately he'll start chopping, whittling, or sawing on something as though obeying an instinct to pick up where Daniel Boone left off.

A fishing companion of mine, annoyed by all the would-be pioneers he finds in the woods, tries to avoid designated wilderness, state parks, and established campgrounds with every opportunity. He has another notion of wilderness, the classic vision—a big stretch of wild country with no particular title, uncut, undeveloped, and most of all, unpeopled. The important thing to him from a philosophical standpoint is that the land is wild, not because government laid down a law, but because the region is so remote no one has bothered to go there. It is protected by a frontier rather than by designation. The main point on the practical side is that there are few other people to contend with in a region that is truly remote, and the ones who are there must have a deep love for wilderness and solitude to have ventured so far into the bush. The only way to enter my friend's wilderness is by canoe or float plane, and most of us can't afford the planes.

Most of us, unfortunately, can't afford to canoe there either. My friend and I both know where such places may be—up along Hudson Bay, in Canada's Northwest Territories, across the northern Rockies, and into Alaska. But have we ever been there? I don't believe my friend has. I never have, and though I would like to take a trip to such a place, I would have to cherish it always, for I don't think I would get many chances to refresh my memory.

And what is happening to these regions? Already in Alaska the pressure to develop, expand, and consume is terrific, and the aura of wilderness—of untouched and untouchable land—is being stripped away by government acronyms, management plans, regulations, and political battles. But if that is bad, what is the alternative?

I don't think there is one.

The late Sigurd Olson, the Ely writer who through the years became the spokesperson for the preservation of the Boundary Waters Canoe Area, first came to border country in 1920 and began guiding two years later. In those days, he once told me, "If you saw another party on the lake, you'd be very disappointed." I asked him whether sometimes the designation of an area such as the Boundary Waters defeats its purpose by inviting ever more people. He had thought about the problem often, and his answer was prompt and firm. "Once you set the area aside you can work out the problem, regulate the use, later," he said. "God, I hate to use that word 'regulation,' but if the area wasn't loved to death, if it wasn't protected, you'd have logging, you'd have mining. God knows what you'd have."

Now, instead of frontier, we have lines on paper and books of regulations. Instead of true wilderness, we have areas managed as wilderness. It's time we accept that, for unless we do, there will be no wilderness at all. The frontier ethic should be allowed to go the way of the frontier. Instead, we need a wilderness ethic.

What is this new ethic? I'm unable to say exactly. But its foundation is ecology, its primary characteristic foresight, and its origin is a great fear, rooted deep in the gut, that the places we treasure will be changed irrevocably by the momentum of our productive, consumptive society.

Though sometimes I have little faith that we can save much of the wilderness we have left, I nonetheless believe that, belatedly and ever so slowly, we are embracing a wilderness ethic. Many recent, controversial battles fought over the Boundary Waters have focused on issues unimaginable a few decades ago—motor use, crowding, and the Neanderthal as camper. Although all these issues have some relation to the environment, they are environmental problems only in the broadest sense. They are aesthetic matters—threats to sensibilities. I personally don't think the preservation of canoe country hangs on a thread so thin it would have broken had we continued to allow motorboats. There are more important environmental concerns. But, that such a question could be argued so vociferously and doggedly tells me that people believe in a spirit of wilderness with passion enough to raise hell. I only hope we have that mettle and those beliefs as we encounter the more crucial issues facing a land we cherish.

95

Left— **Ski trails**